— THE —
MISSING
SEMESTER

— THE —
MISSING
SEMESTER

MATT KABALA
GENE NATALI

The Missing Semester

HARRIMAN HOUSE LTD
3 Viceroy Court
Bedford Road
Petersfield
Hampshire
GU32 3LJ
GREAT BRITAIN
Tel: +44 (0)1730 233870

Email: enquiries@harriman-house.com
Website: harriman.house

This edition published in 2022 by Harriman House
Copyright © 2020 The Missing Semester, LLC

The right of The Missing Semester, LLC to be identified as the Author has been asserted in accordance with the Copyright, Design and Patents Act 1988.

Paperback ISBN: 978-0-85719-980-5
eBook ISBN: 978-0-85719-981-2

British Library Cataloguing in Publication Data
A CIP catalogue record for this book can be obtained from the British Library.

Cover design by Brian Taylor
Interior book design and layout by Hunt Smith Design

To Nolan, Cailyn, Taylor, Maddie, Kiley & Jason,

We began writing with the hope that this book would touch the lives of many, but with the expectation that it would be read just by you. Wishing you the courage to chase your own dreams, the passion to make them come true, and the determination to see that they do.

TABLE OF CONTENTS

YOUR CHOICES HAVE CONSEQUENCES
WILL YOU CHOOSE WISELY?

Most people you know probably won't read this book. Some might read it and ignore the advice that it offers. Some will think it doesn't apply to their circumstances, or that they already *know this stuff*. The point is, each of us is different, and we think our individual financial paths unique.

But are they?

Statistics tell a different and very dismal story about the financial decisions that we make throughout our lives, and we present those stats in the ensuing chapters. They tell us that as a population we generally make poor financial decisions—and have a lot of excuses for making them. Our own schooling provided the evidence that the system does not prepare us for the financial decisions that we face after high school, college, trade school, or graduate school. And *our* classes focused on business and finance!

Take responsibility early and you will be better off later.

We try to provide a little experience-based guidance, and stress that *your financial decisions from a very early point in your life can have long-term effects.* Whether those effects are good or bad depends on the choices that you make. We try hard to make the point that *you are responsible for your decisions, and are therefore in control of the outcome.*

Gene & Matt

CHAPTER 1
WHY THIS FINANCIAL STUFF MATTERS

Are you ready?

This book is about money stuff—financial matters and financial decisions that will have a profound effect on your life. You can learn about this stuff and reap the considerable benefits . . . or skip this semester and suffer the consequences. You might not get these subjects in school, and they don't usually make for locker-room or water-cooler conversation. But they affect critical decisions almost all of us face. Still, there are topics here many people hesitate to discuss—maybe because they don't know the right questions to ask, or because they don't realize they are *already making* choices with potentially big consequences.

If this applies to you, you are not alone. What we talk about here is based on our personal experiences as well as the real-life experiences of many others, people probably just like you. We can't promise to rid you of worries about issues like debt, income, and financial obligations. We *can* help you avoid pitfalls and see opportunities. Start today. Why today? Because it's expensive to wait, as you'll see.

Consider a few facts about our collective financial life:

77% of Americans are stressed over finances.[1]

69% of Americans live paycheck-to-paycheck.[2]

54% of American households spend more than they earn each year.[3]

Student debt increased to an estimated 1.5 TRILLION dollars in 2020.[4]

The sticker price of a college education has increased 370% over the last thirty two years.[5]

Total credit card debt is approaching one TRILLION dollars.[6]

Much of our education system is designed to prepare us for careers in specific fields, and most institutions do an exemplary job of that. But few, if any, teach us "how to live" in relation to money. Take the plight of a physical therapist whom we interviewed for this book. After seven years of school to gain hard-earned undergraduate and doctorate degrees, her starting salary limited her ability to live on her own and repay her student loans. Anyone with a modest salary facing seven years' worth of college debt would be similarly challenged. This problem should have been addressed seven years ago! The flaw in this case, or in the curriculum, was in the lack of preparation for life after school. But don't panic. Your education might not have prepared you for life's financial challenges, but it doesn't prohibit you from making good, disciplined decisions. We can grumble that school hasn't prepared us for financial life, or we can do something about it. Remember, hope, while important, is not a plan. *A course of action* is.

Begin by briefing yourself on the basics. Take control of your financial life today. Ignore the financial basics and risk paying the future consequences (you'll only be able to blame yourself).

Consider this a book about *how to avoid big problems.* It starts with a short course on managing **spending and earnings.** Postponing discussion of a job, it digs first into **debt,** since most graduates, with or without an income now, left school with debt of one kind or another. In any case, this book isn't a job guide. Although, after discussing debt we'll address financial decisions about your job and your income, then go on to **investing, housing,** and finally, preparing for the long term, **retirement.**

The "missing semester" that follows is not a tough one, but it's arguably the most important semester of all. We hope it helps to prepare you for what's ahead.

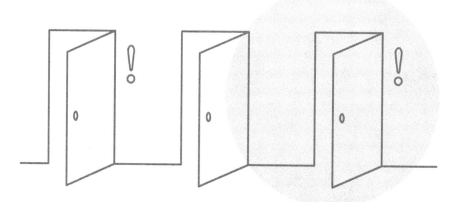

CHAPTER 2
THE REST OF YOUR LIFE STARTS NOW

Are you prepared for "life" after college?

> **Authors' note:** *If you chose to bypass college in favor of trade school, military service, or any number of other possibilities—please read on. The information that follows still applies.*

Over 1.9 million students graduated with bachelor's degrees from U.S. colleges in 2020, and for many of these now young professionals, the world just got narrower.[7] This might seem counter-intuitive; and to an extent, it is. Most of your school life you heard that the world would be at your fingertips after college, and that you would be able to do what you want. This sounds nice, but the reality is that *responsibility* takes precedence—responsibility to provide for yourself and to fulfill past promises. College is over, and the next semester of your life begins now. Welcome to the real world! At the outset, let us offer a simple formula worth remembering and repeating to yourself, often.

Do not let your spending dictate your saving.

You'll hear this again from us.

If you are like most graduates, and many non-graduates and not-yet-graduates, the elephant in the room at this point in your life is debt, probably in the form of student loans (and likely credit cards). If you are an "average" 2019 graduate, your student loans total over $29,200[8] and your unpaid credit card balance totals $2,351.[9] It is your responsibility to repay these debts; and the consequences of not paying are severe. That is one reason the world just got more narrow.

While spending more for your education does not necessarily translate to a better education, more opportunities, or even a higher salary, that's irrelevant now. The cost of your education has become what businesses refer to as a *sunk cost*. It is money that has already been spent. You don't need to be reminded that a college education is not free. Nor, for that matter, is it cheap.

When you choose to pursue a formal education, colleges agree to provide it in exchange for tuition that is often manageable only by borrowing money in the form of student loans. We will address this subject (and your credit cards) in greater detail later in this book. But for starters, in order to eliminate debt, you need income. And if, in addition to eliminating debt, you have the audacity to want food, shelter, clothing, and transportation, then you had better prepare accordingly.

The average starting salary for 2019 college graduates was $51,000.[10] Clearly this amount—bumped up by a few in high-start fields—is a considerable sum. Whether your salary is smaller, or larger, the question is *"what do I do with it?"* For an answer, it's helpful to examine how the average American spends his or her income.

The following pie chart shows our spending habits as a nation.

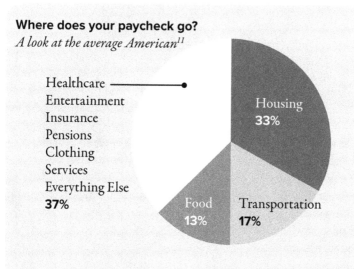

Where does your paycheck go?
A look at the average American[11]

Healthcare ●——————
Entertainment
Insurance
Pensions
Clothing
Services
Everything Else
37%

Housing
33%

Food
13%

Transportation
17%

Looking at these numbers, you can see that the necessities of food, transportation, and shelter, represent a substantial percentage of our spending. These three consume 63% of the average American's after tax annual income! *You can expect the same.* But, neither taxes nor student loan payments are included in the pie chart. Remember, the average 2019 college graduate is responsible for the repayment of over $29,200 in school loans. Using a student loan interest rate of 6%, repayment of that average comes to $324 each month for the next ten years, or $3,890 a year!

MONTHLY EXPENSES, AFTER TAXES
(based on averages)

Housing (33% of income)	$1,109
Transportation (17%)	$578
Food (13%)	$439
Insurance/Pensions (11%)	$385
Healthcare (8%)	$277
Entertainment (5%)	$162
Clothing & Services (3%)	$101
Everything Else (10%)	$329
TOTAL	$3,380

Remember that $324 you owe for student loans every month?

For an estimate of your spending power in actual dollars when you include student loan responsibilities, look at the list of **monthly expenses** above. It applies the percentages from the pie chart you saw on the previous page to that average starting salary of $51,000 mentioned at the beginning of the chapter. That salary equates to a monthly take-home pay of $3,380 (after income taxes, Social Security, Medicare, etc.).[12] So if your monthly income is $3,380, the list shows how much of that total will go to each expense, if you match the average. If your income is smaller, you'll have to reduce each expense on your list proportionally.

The value of this exercise is three-fold. It gives a glimpse of the big picture—that is, the financial challenges we all face. More specifically, it points out potential problem areas that might be unique to you as an individual. Finally, it shows how little room there is for error.

Assuming you already have a job, there are a couple of ways to increase your actual end-of-the-month income. You can pursue the obvious and try to earn more money. Less evident, but very effective and perhaps quicker, is to spend less. In combination, the two are powerful.

MANAGE YOUR EXPENSES

For example, if you are paying more than "average" for a house or apartment (more than 33% of your income), you are likely having to make sacrifices elsewhere. Housing costs can be reduced substantially by living with friends or family and sharing the cost. The same exercise also helps you to identify other areas for potential savings. In the list of expenses the amount budgeted for entertainment each month is $162. Maybe it's possible to save an extra $50 a month by eating in instead of dining out, or by cutting back on other entertainment. Doing that for the full year generates $600 in extra savings. It may not sound like much, but as you will see later, that $600 in savings is a big deal! This is just one example. Areas for potential savings will be different for everyone.

While the latest tech toy or fashion trend may seem irresistible, make a practice of asking yourself the core questions.

Do I need it? If yes, Why?

You might be surprised. These two simple but important questions will save you money (not to mention headaches) in the years to come. So taking a look at your monthly budget deserves a few minutes of your time.

Remember that $324 you owe each month for your student loans? Take a look back at the monthly expense list and you will see that little obligation eliminates the majority of your discretionary income—much of the *Everything else* category. A real eye-opener, wouldn't you agree? And data suggest that it takes college graduates between 10 and 30 years to pay off their student loans.[13] Now, remember *the best advice you never got* (before you started this chapter, anyway).

Make your saving dictate your spending, not the reverse.

And its companion,

Manage spending to maximize savings.

Making an informed decision to save money (starting now) is perhaps the most important one that you can make at this point in your life.

CHAPTER 3
UNDERSTANDING DEBT

How much do you really know about debt?

Debt

It's a fundamental feature of the national and global economy. For businesses, debt is an important source of capital, sometimes creating the opportunity for companies to grow at faster rates than they could without borrowing. For individuals, debt is a tool (if used wisely) that can help us achieve a quality of life that might otherwise be unobtainable.

Every spring, high school seniors nationwide make the decision that the potential benefits of a college degree outweigh the known costs of tuition and any necessary student loans. Another example of debt's value might apply to someone who forgoes college to start a small business. In this case, a loan from the local bank (or, more likely, from friends and family) can help to get this new business up and running. A third example is buying a house. For most Americans, home ownership would not be possible without the availability of mortgage loans. Despite these perfectly valid reasons for borrowing money, debt remains a source of stress and frustration for many Americans because it is often misused. The worst case of misuse is for instant gratification.

Yes, debt is a valuable tool, but a tool that must be used appropriately and wisely. If abused, it can be very dangerous. This is because with debt comes uncertainty, but it is uncertainty backed by a powerful obligation, legal and moral, to repay—whatever the use. Make no mistake, the responsibility of managing and paying off your debt is squarely on your shoulders.

Here's one important rule for approaching debt wisely.

Do not let your lifestyle determine your debt.

Instead, let your debt determine your lifestyle. **If you are paying back student loans and credit cards, you should be cutting other expenses.** This means eliminating unnecessary purchases. Remember those two core questions about purchases? **Do I need it?** If so, **Why?** Wisely, you'll be asking those questions about the latest technology, a new car, how to furnish your apartment, or any other component of a costly lifestyle.

Your aim should be to pay off your debt as quickly and efficiently as possible. Why?

Less debt = More freedom

That's freedom to live independently, to make your own choices. For most of us, having more personal debt means having less personal freedom. As crazy as it sounds, the quality of your life can be largely determined by the amount of debt you have.

Here are four keys to preserving your freedom.

1

● **KNOW YOUR DEBT**

For example, if you have student loans, do you know when they mature? Should some types of debt be repaid before others? Do you know when you must begin making payments? How much are the monthly payments? What are your interest rates? Are the interest rates fixed or can they increase over time?

MANAGE YOUR DEBT
● **Not borrowing more than you can repay is the cardinal rule.** (Remember the **Monthly Expenses** list from Chapter 2?) Borrowing too much will burden you with minimum payments, higher interest rates, and large interest payments for years to come, greatly reducing your personal and financial freedom. Taking on too much debt can damage your credit score if repayment becomes an issue.

3. HAVE ONLY ONE CREDIT CARD

This is an easy rule to follow. We will address this topic in greater depth in a later chapter.

4. UNDERSTAND PRINCIPAL AND INTEREST

This is a very simple concept that is too often overlooked. The vast majority of borrowers look only at the total monthly payment. Especially if you are young, this is the first step down a very slippery slope. Understand the difference between principal and interest. The quicker you pay off the principal, the less you pay in interest. The less you pay in interest, the less you pay overall. Remember, **larger (voluntary) debt payments = less interest.**

Loan words to know

The **principal** of a loan is the amount borrowed. *For example, a $10,000 student loan requires that you repay $10,000 in principal.*

Interest is what a lender charges a borrower for a loan. *For example, a 6% annual interest rate on your loan requires that you pay an extra $3,323 in interest payments over the life of that $10,000 ten-year loan.*

The **monthly payment** is based on the original loan plus the agreed-upon interest rate.

Overall payment is the sum total of interest and principal over the life of the loan.

The next chapters focus on four primary types of debt: student loans, credit cards, auto loans, and later, home loans (mortgages). For now, **recognize that while borrowing money is common and sometimes advantageous, it is not a decision to be taken lightly.** Be smart, not clever, about managing your debt. A loan is a legal obligation, with all the possible consequences that implies. Manage your budget. Be frugal. Live within your means.

CHAPTER 4
STUDENT LOANS

Do you have a plan for managing them?

College is widely perceived to be the most effective path to career and financial success. That might or might not be the case, but this perception has enabled universities across the country to raise tuition an astounding 370% over the last thirty years . . . without losing students! Given these huge increases in tuition, it's no surprise that Americans are borrowing more than ever for student loans. Total student loans outstanding (borrowed but not yet repaid) surpassed 1.5 trillion dollars in 2019.

Repaying your part of that 1.5 trillion dollars is an obligation you must address immediately, and it can be daunting. Welcome to life after school. There is no changing that promissory note you signed four years ago. You made a commitment in exchange for a college education, and your *alma mater* has already delivered on its end of the deal by granting your diploma (one hopes). Regardless of whether or not you still think it was a fair trade, it's time to make good on your promise.

Here's one approach.

"I want to quickly eliminate some of my loans. I have one $10,000 loan with an 8.0% interest rate and two smaller $2,000 loans at 4.0%. I have been paying off the $2,000 loans so that I will have fewer loans to repay."

—RECENT GRADUATE

Is this smart? While this approach might seem the least painful, the false sense of accomplishment is just that. The **interest rate,** not the size of the loan, should determine which loan you address first.

Pay off high-interest-rate loans first.

At the same time, any steps you can take to lower the amount of your interest payment(s) will ultimately *reduce* your overall payment. *Overall payment,* you recall, is the total of all interest and principal payments over the life of a loan. Never lose sight of that big picture. A lower interest rate enables you to contribute more of your income to principal payments (reducing your debt) while making the same payment (that is, writing the same-size check). In many instances, you might be able to lower your total interest rate by consolidating your student loans (combining multiple loans into a single loan).

In any case, reducing the interest you pay by paying off high-interest loans first is the smart course of action. The sooner you eliminate your student debt, the sooner you will be on your way to financial freedom. That assumes, of course, you make the sensible choice not to increase your other debt. (Remember, *only one credit card.*)

Minimum payment. Let's examine this next. The minimum payment on your student loan (as with any type of borrowing, such as your credit card) is the minimum dollar amount that you must pay each month to the provider of your loans (the company, institution, or person that loaned you money to pay tuition). Make no mistake: you are required to make at least the minimum payment each month. But have you ever asked, What is the maximum payment I'm allowed to make? This is an excellent question. The answer is,

There is no maximum payment.

If you have the means, you can repay your entire loan in one payment. Okay, that's probably unlikely. But we strongly encourage you to pay the maximum dollar amount that you can afford each month. Every time you pay more than the minimum, those extra dollars pay off principal, which means that over the life of the loan you will pay back less in total. (Remember that **big picture?**)

Paying more than the minimum. To emphasize the value of this strategy, let's take a look at two examples involving a $10,000 loan with an 8% interest rate and $100 minimum payment. First, look at the benefits of *consistently* paying more than the minimum monthly payment.

EFFECTS OF INCREASED REGULAR PAYMENTS
$10,000 loan, 8% interest, $100/month

PAYMENT	AMOUNT	TOTAL NUMBER OF MONTHLY PAYMENTS	TOTAL INTEREST PAID OVER THE LIFE OF LOAN
minimum	$100	166	$6,534
twice the minimum	$200	62	$2,204
three times the minimum	$300	38	$1,347
five times the minimum	$500	22	$769

Note that there are *two big benefits* of paying more than the minimum each month: lower total interest payments and less time until the loan is repaid in full. **Remember that $50 a month in savings (from eating in) from Chapter 2?** This is one place you can put that money to work!

Now look at the benefits of just a *one-time* extra loan payment—that is, paying more than the minimum in just a single month. For instance, you might forgo an unnecessary purchase (a new ski jacket, say) and instead use that money to make a larger loan payment. In the second example, you wisely decide against purchasing that new ski jacket in *month two* of the repayment plan. Instead, you use that money ($100, $200, or $400, depending on which jacket you do not buy) to increase that month's payment toward your student loans.

EFFECTS OF A ONE-TIME INCREASED PAYMENT
$10,000 loan, 8% interest, $100/month

PAYMENT	TOTAL NUMBER OF MONTHLY PAYMENTS	TOTAL INTEREST PAID OVER THE LIFE OF LOAN	SAVINGS
minimum monthly payment only	166	$6,534	—
minimum + one-time payment of $100	163	$6,340	*$194*
minimum + one-time payment of $200	160	$6,152	*$382*
minimum + one-time payment of $400	154	$5,791	*$743*

From this table you can see that **just a single, one-time higher principal payment can have an extremely positive effect on your overall loan repayment.** Not spending, say, $200 for that jacket—and instead adding that amount to the $100 minimum-payment amount for a single month, saved our skier $382 over the life of the loan and shortened the total payment period by three months (even if he or she makes only the minimum payment every month afterwards). When you look at it this way, that ski jacket is even more expensive. Is it worth it?

Student loans are often necessary, but it helps to know that there are ways to reduce your interest payments, your overall payment, and the number of months or years until the loan is repaid. Every dollar you cut from interest payments is a dollar available to save or spend elsewhere.

CHAPTER 5
CREDIT CARD(S)

How many do you have?
How many do you need?

Credit cards can be a valuable tool *if used wisely*. Correction: **one** credit card can be a valuable tool *if used wisely*. And that means you should **never** carry a balance from one month to the next. Instead, pay off the full balance each month. A credit-card balance carried to the next month is the most punishing form of borrowing. This seemingly harmless piece of plastic can become a serious threat to your financial well-being. Credit cards and the agreement you sign accepting their terms are widely misunderstood. (Yes, you do sign an agreement!) As a result, cardholders often make unwise decisions.

Student #1: Can I pay more than the minimum on my credit card?

Student #2: Yeah, I did that one time.

Let's discuss the matter in greater detail so that you are better informed and can avoid the common traps.

Don't misunderstand us: there are good reasons to have a credit card. Responsible use of a credit card can be a good way to establish your credit history. Rewards programs might be attractive in terms of free travel and other incentives if you manage your credit properly (that is, pay off your entire balance every month). And credit cards can provide a good source of emergency funds should you need them. Let's face it, emergencies happen, and sometimes credit cards are the only option, despite their drawbacks.

Yes, these pieces of plastic can be helpful. **However, caution and awareness of consequences are essential.** For instance, if you make only the *minimum* monthly payment (2% of outstanding balance in this example), do you know how long will it take to pay off a $5,000 credit card balance with a 20% interest rate (not uncommon)? As unbelievable as it sounds, it will take you more than 56 years![14] And that's assuming you don't make a single additional purchase during those 56 years. Even more frightening, that $5,000 balance will cost you another $22,126.13 in interest payments. So that $5,000 in purchases really cost you $27,126.13! Frightening? Certainly. A little unrealistic? Perhaps. But not as much as you might think.

The average outstanding credit card balance in the U.S. in 2020 is $6,200.[15]

If you pay $100 every month (rather than just the minimum monthly payment) on that $5,000 balance, you will shorten the life of your loan to nine years, and $5,840 in extra interest. Still painful.

Credit card companies are required to include a table with this same *"more than the minimum"* math on every monthly statement sent to cardholders. Like the tables about student loans in Chapter 4, the table on the credit card statement shows the benefit of paying more than the minimum each month.

Sometimes it is necessary to walk before we run. When debt is uncomfortably high, every painful step counts. But the pain can be temporary. Make the sacrifices necessary to live within your means. The table on your credit card statement showing the benefit of making more than the minimum payment does not indicate that there is another choice, simply living within your means. The best approach is unchanged and inarguable: avoid interest penalties altogether and

Pay off your credit card balance **in full** each month.

Many Americans have become personally familiar with the dangers of credit card debt. Excessive credit card debt easily (and quickly) becomes an endless cycle of frustration and worry that will cost you thousands of dollars and many sleepless nights. **There are a few simple rules to keep in mind when using credit cards.**

1. PAY YOUR ENTIRE BALANCE EVERY MONTH

There is a commonly held misconception that in order to maintain a positive credit score you need to carry a balance on your credit card. *This is false.* You should pay off your credit card balance in its entirety every month. Do not carry a balance from month to month. If you do, you will be charged interest (probably very high interest) on the unpaid balance.

2. AVOID USING CREDIT TO PAY OFF CREDIT

Balance transfers (paying off one balance with funds borrowed from another source) are nothing but a short-term solution to a bigger problem. Don't fall into this ugly cycle. Adjust your saving and spending and reduce your debt. A possible exception to this rule: consolidating loans (combining several debts into a single loan) can make sense *if it reduces your overall payment*— the total amount of interest, principal and any fees over the life of the loan. But get all the info and numbers first.

3.

IF YOU CAN'T PAY THE FULL BALANCE IN A GIVEN MONTH, PAY AS MUCH AS YOU CAN

Paying as much as possible every month reduces the financial pain of additional interest charges. You don't want your hard-earned money going toward interest payments. The more you pay each month, the sooner you will be debt-free. After all, that's the goal, isn't it?

These simple rules will save you time, money, and anguish. A credit card used inappropriately and without caution can become a part of your established credit rating. Mistakes today are documented and can make it more difficult and more expensive to borrow later— say, for a car or a house. Remember, your choices have consequences.

Afterthought

Pay off your highest-interest debt first (as Chapter 4 urged in connection with student loans). For example, suppose you have credit-card debt with a 13% interest rate and student loans with an 8% rate. Which to repay first?

In this case, pay off the credit card debt first. Its 13% rate is adding more to your interest cost per dollar of debt than the 8% rate on your student loans. Lower your interest rate and you'll lower your overall loan payment (**the big picture** *again*). You also will likely receive a tax deduction on your student loan interest payments which you do not receive with credit card payments.

CHAPTER 6
LET'S TALK ABOUT CAR LOANS

New car, used car . . . or no car at all?

Everyone drives a used car—and don't let anyone tell you differently. The minute the buyer drives a new car off the lot it becomes a used car, and the immediate (and substantial) drop in the car's value reflects this harsh reality.

So let's talk about cars. If you live in a city that allows you to live without a car, seriously consider doing so. Living vehicle-free is a great way to save your hard-earned dollars.

Your first car should be a hand-me-down that's held together with duct tape. Well, not really. But joking aside, the purpose of your first car is to get you safely and reliably from *Point A* to *Point B*—nothing else.

Contrary to popular belief and practice, the purpose of your first car **is not** to impress your friends. Nor should it help put you on the road to money problems. Give that used hunk of metal a cool name and drive it into the ground. The memories will be priceless and that car will make for great stories later in life. In addition, you will have taken an important step towards financial freedom. The money you save can be spent in other ways (loan reduction, savings, investments, even the perfect date). Your friends who couldn't resist the urge to splurge on the newest sports car probably won't be so fortunate. This is not the time in life to fall into the trap of trying to impress the people around you. In time, your peers will respect your work ethic and ability to make smart, disciplined decisions more than the car you drive. The goal should be to build wealth, not maintain its appearance.

If you are fortunate enough to have an extra $200-$400 sitting around each month, the advice remains the same: be smart about purchasing a car. Count your blessings, and buy the less expensive vehicle. This is an opportunity to get a head start financially on the rest of your life. Understanding the effect of interest rates is one way to get that head start.

EFFECT OF INTEREST RATES
Five-year, $15,000 auto loan

INTEREST RATE	MONTHLY PAYMENT	TOTAL PAYMENT	DIFFERENCE (COST OF INTEREST)
0%	$250	$15,000	—
3%	$270	$16,170	*$1,170*
5%	$283	$16,985	*$1,985*
7%	$297	$17,821	*$2,821*
10%	$319	$19,122	$4,122

This **$4,122 could be better spent elsewhere.** *Never underestimate the impact of interest rates. Know the* **real** *cost before making a purchase of this magnitude!*

But that's all there is to it, right? Walk into the dealership, negotiate to buy the car for $15,000, arrange for a low interest rate, and buy the car. Absolutely not!

So what is the real cost of owning a car? First you have the unavoidable closing costs and sales tax. Second is the interest-rate effect (outlined in detail in the preceding table). We'll assume that $15k didn't come from under your pillow, and that you are financing (borrowing to pay for) or leasing the vehicle. And don't forget maintenance and upkeep. Oh, yes, and insurance. The monthly payment is far from the only cost associated with owning a car. Your commute to work alone can cost $100 a month. Insurance will probably cost an additional $100 a month, if not more, and it can take years of accident-free driving before that cost decreases. Routine maintenance (such as oil changes), taxes, and state inspection (where required) can add another $200-300, at least, to the annual cost of car ownership. Now add the cost of new tires, engine tune-ups, brake pads, and other fixes. These are all expenses you will face—likely after the warranty expires. They are part of the real cost of owning a car, and you cannot ignore this total cost when deciding whether to buy a car.

Of course, many people don't have the option of living without a vehicle. So how do you manage? The obvious answer is to not buy a car that you can't afford. Less obvious, however, is *knowing how much is too much*. The temptation to overspend is much higher when you are blinded by the spotlight reflecting off the hood of that brand new car on the dealer's showroom floor. Wear sunglasses when you go, and prepare before you shop. Here are some steps that might help you prepare.

Step 1: **Know how much car you can afford**
This requires little explanation. If you are someone who has to have the latest sports car, and you can *"afford"* it only by living in your parents' basement, now is an appropriate time to re-examine your understanding of the word *afford*.

Step 2: **Don't buy more car than you can afford**
This is not the time to purchase the car of your dreams. A five-year auto loan of $30,000 at 7% interest will cost you an additional $5,643 in interest payments—bringing the total cost of that loan to $35,643 (assuming you make monthly payments). Do you have an extra $5,643 to shell out for interest payments? That's money that could have been spent on repaying your student loans, paying rent, even building investments.

Step 3: **All else being equal, buy the car with the lower interest rate**
Many auto finance companies will entice you with a reduced monthly payment—along with a longer loan term in the fine print. Resist the temptation to accept this "deal." That extra year or two of indebtedness will only cost you more money in interest payments. Don't buy based on *monthly* payment; buy on the *calculated* total cost you can afford.

The longer you finance, the more interest you will pay.

There is one important exception to this rule. If you qualify for a zero-interest loan, negotiate for the longest financing term option available. If you personally do not qualify, explore the possibility of having a family member who does qualify co-sign the loan for you. Remember from Chapter 3 that the interest you pay on your auto loan is the cost of borrowing money. In the case of a 0% loan (all else, including the price of the car, being the same) you are borrowing for free. If you do qualify for a zero- or low-interest loan, fight the temptation to buy more car than you need. Instead, buy a less expensive and more practical car. If you happen to be a car enthusiast and the thought of not having your dream car keeps you awake at night, consider this a temporary sacrifice. By resisting the temptation to purchase the car of your dreams today, you will be more financially secure—and better equipped to buy (and afford) that dream car—down the road. (More on this in *The Missing Second Semester*.)

For some readers, this discussion on cars is a moot point simply because it's far more convenient to live vehicle-free (think New York City). But let's say you are one of those people who doesn't have the option of living without a car. In some places and under some circumstances, it simply isn't possible. If you must have a vehicle for your daily commute, seek assistance in finding the most competitive loan rates. Carefully research all available options before you make a decision. Remember that immediate drop in value mentioned at the beginning of the chapter?

The value of a new car drops by 20% the instant you drive off the lot.

Your new $15,000 car? It's now worth $12,000 and you haven't even made it home! Does your loan balance reflect that immediate depreciation? Nope. You still must pay off the entire loan on the car you bought for $15,000 but that's now sadly only worth $12,000. Can you think of an easier or faster way to make your money disappear? And this is just a start; that new car will lose 40% of its resale value in only three years.[16]

Which brings us to some of the benefits of a used car:[17]

Lower purchase price

Lower depreciation (the decline in its dollar value)

Lower registration and licensing fees in some states

Lower insurance premiums

Yes, maintenance costs might be higher, so make sure you do your research before purchasing.

Buying your first car (or your tenth) can be fun, exciting, and a little scary and overwhelming. The temptation to spend more than you should can be high. Don't let this distract you from the primary objective: *your* financial well-being. Buy a used vehicle. You won't regret it. Remember, *everyone drives a used car.*

CHAPTER 7
TAKE OWNERSHIP
OF YOUR FUTURE

What kind of life do you want to have?

Okay, enough about debt. Let's now focus on getting the income to pay it off and building financial security for the days and years ahead.

By now you know the financial choices you make today have consequences. But a remarkably sophisticated, rational decision-making capability is one of the distinguishing features of human beings. Every day, we are faced with, and make, hundreds (if not thousands) of decisions. While most are not life-changing, some will affect you for the rest of your life. **The decision to manage your finances, and lifestyle, is one of the best decisions you can make.** As we have argued, this is a critical period in your life. Yes, there are obstacles in your way, but there are opportunities as well.

Imagine for a moment that you are someone else—more than a century ago (true story).

In 1902 at the age of 17 with nothing more than the clothes on his back, $7.50 in his pocket, and the promise of a better future, Daliso left his home in Tuscany, Italy, and embarked on a journey that changed his life. Daliso came to America. He was seeking opportunity and he found it. First as a coal miner in Pittsburgh, Pennsylvania, and then, after he married, as a butcher at his wife's family store. Daliso recognized the importance of a paycheck, and this awareness allowed him to realize his dream of supporting a family. Daliso and his wife raised four children (two doctors, an engineer and a teacher). Suffice it to say, that $7.50 went a long way.

Starting without enough to treat his family to a round of Starbucks coffees today, Daliso succeeded in changing his life and shaping his future. (Okay, that $7.50 would have bought a month's worth of fancy coffees in 1902, but not a whole lot more.) How did he do it? How did he build the life he wanted? Certainly **hard work, perseverance, and discipline** were essential. In combination, these traits are a formula for success—one that has been tested repeatedly. It works! Unlike our friend Daliso, who did everything, *everything* he could to ensure a steady income, many recent graduates now decide to hold out for a "better job" or the "right opportunity." Waiting for a better job *only* makes sense if you are already working. **A steady paycheck is always better than no paycheck,** and

Any job is better than **no** job.

Sure, while you are waiting for that "right" opportunity, you might have to work two or even three less-desirable jobs just to make ends meet. This is unquestionably the right approach. There is no shame in earning an honest paycheck, however small. **The real mistake is choosing to earn zero dollars because it doesn't match your expectations or because you consider yourself over-qualified for an open position.** Be proud, but also be humble and practical.

Without a paycheck, you can dream about your future. With a paycheck, you can build it.

Recognizing that your financial security is *your* responsibility is essential to making your dream a reality. The sooner you start, the better your odds of achieving it. Failure to acknowledge that responsibility, to make the necessary decisions, and to take the necessary actions may be the reason 69% of Americans live paycheck-to-paycheck, barely getting by, one step from financial trouble. *Sixty-nine percent!* You must avoid this trap.

"I arrived home at midnight on Wednesday and was surprised to see a moving van in front of my neighbor's house. A moving van? At midnight? I walked over and asked why they were moving. They told me the bank had foreclosed on the house. I was sad and speechless. They had two cars in the driveway, and I could see the TV on through the window. The bank listed the house at $60,000! I found myself wondering why they didn't cut the cable or sell one of the cars to keep their home a little longer."

— A NEIGHBOR

This is a reminder of the need to take responsibility for one's own financial well-being. Many of the things we take for granted (two cars and cable TV, for example) are not necessities, nor are they entitlements. Cable television is a luxury, to be paid for by work and spare income. Selling one car and cutting the cable bill might have bought this family an additional 12 months in their home, maybe more.

The lesson? Weigh needs against wants. If done correctly, setting priorities and questioning wants (*Do I need it? Why?*) can also be your ticket to a vacation. On a more positive note:

"Cable? Are you crazy? I save $1,200 a year by not having cable! I invest some of it and the rest I save for a plane ticket and ski trip!"

— PHYSICIAN'S ASSISTANT AT CHILDREN'S HOSPITAL, PITTSBURGH

CHAPTER 8
COST-EFFECTIVE CAREER MOVES

Have you considered ways to complement the classroom—or your job?

But a remarkably sophisticated, rational decision-making capability is one of the distinguishing features of human beings. (from Chapter 7)

No small part of those human capabilities is the capacity to second-guess ourselves, re-evaluate the decisions we make, and at times, change our mind. Let's be honest, we have all been wrong, many times. Consider that 71% of college graduates stay in their first job for less than a year.[18] With that in mind, **does it make sense to spend thousands of dollars and years of effort on an advanced degree that might be significantly less valuable in a few years if you change careers?** The question is imperative because many college students use graduate school as the *"fallback"* plan after graduation. Under this *"fallback"* plan, you replace the *income* from a first job with the *expense* of graduate school. Consider whether you want to risk flushing away tens of thousands of dollars and two or three years because you haven't made up your mind about a career.

The landscaping company that a landlord hired for a small multi-unit apartment building was run by a man in his thirties who had previously attended and paid for a master's degree from a highly-ranked business school. Soon after graduation the young man decided to switch careers, and he started a small landscaping business.

Does it make sense to spend $100,000 on a master's degree if you are *uncertain* about your career choice? Sure, some of what one learns in an MBA program might have value for a landscaping career, but that's unlikely to be an efficient use of time and money. Might it not make more sense to gain some experience before making a sizable financial and time commitment to that career? And you might want to give *all* the possibilities of this expensive decision careful thought. **If you decide that graduate school matches your career plans, is it possible to go to school at night so that you can work during the day? Will your employer help pay the cost of tuition?**

Let your career determine your advanced degree, **not the reverse.**

There are cost-effective decisions that will allow you to continue to advance a career and gain experience before investing so much of your money and time in an expensive graduate program. Don't misinterpret this chapter as an attack on higher education. To the contrary, there is no substitute for education. We are simply suggesting that **when it comes to advanced degrees,** *look before you leap.* And maybe test the waters. This approach is especially important for new college graduates already tied down with undergraduate student loans.

THE VALUE OF AN MBA

"There's a joke among some Harvard (Business School) students that there are three S's: study, sleep, and socializing, and that students really only have time for two of the three."

— HARVARD BUSINESS SCHOOL STUDENT QUOTED
  IN THE WALL STREET JOURNAL
  WSJ 2/3/2011

The suggestion is that socializing and networking are more valuable to long-term success in the business world than studying. If that's the case, then it's worth asking: in the era of social media, smartphones, and video chat, does one need to write a $100,000 check in order to socialize for two years?

What if, instead, you networked with professionals across a variety of career fields and learned about different opportunities while continuing to consider a long-term career? It makes sense to be comfortable and confident in your career before choosing to invest in it with more borrowed money. Because education and decisions about it are so important, consider some less-expensive ways to build your résumé and knowledge, and test your interests. The idea is to help further your career and increase your salary while ultimately helping to make the costs of that graduate degree more manageable, should you choose to pursue it.

Professional certifications are a practical alternative and strong complement to a graduate degree. Often overlooked by recent graduates and young professionals, these certifications can help a résumé stand out in a crowd. There are a wide variety of professional certifications. They have value in their respective fields, and in general they are substantially cheaper than a graduate degree.

Professional Certifications

Investments
Chartered Financial Anyalyst (CFA®)

Accounting
Certified Public Accountant (CPA®)

Aviation
Private Pilot License (PPL)
Commercial Pilot License (CPL)

Law
Certified Legal Assistant (CLA®)

Personal Finance
Certified Financial Planner (CFP®)

Information Technology
Cisco Certified Network Associate (CCNA®)

Medicine
Emergency Medical Technician (EMT)

Horticulture
Arborist (ISA® Certified Arborist)

These are only a few of the possibilities, but you get the point. There are far too many career-specific professional certifications to list here. Any one of these credentials demonstrates commitment and determination to potential employers, not to mention know-how and experience. **Don't discount or ignore the value of professional certifications.** Remember,

Look before you leap.

Hope is not a plan. A course of action is.
(from Chapter 1)

In addition to the knowledge gained, pursuit of a professional certification might help you decide if the field fits your interests and talents. If, at the end of the day (okay, months ... maybe years), you do decide on a different career, you have spent a couple thousand dollars on a professional certification as opposed to tens of thousands on an advanced degree. (Did we mention that graduate school is expensive?) In the meantime, those "would-have-been" grad-school dollars could be making their way to your 401(k) or Roth IRA (see Chapter 9), building your financial future. **When time and money are involved, and you don't have more of either than you need, why not take one step at a time as you begin your career?** In doing so, you will help yourself achieve your financial and lifestyle goals.

Give your career a test drive
In many states it is possible to become an Emergency Medical Technician or Paramedic at no cost by volunteering with a local ambulance service or fire department. Working on an ambulance and responding to medical emergencies is one way to "test out" the medical field. Better to know if health care is for you before investing money and years of your life in nursing or medical school.

There are many ways to build your knowledge base that do not require a risky financial commitment. Volunteering as an Emergency Medical Technician is just one example. In addition to pursuing certifications and relevant work experience, there's an even more cost-effective course of action. **Take the time to talk with—and listen to—people with experience in the fields you are considering.** An alumni network, a university career database, a career counselor, family and friends are all good starting points to get in touch with someone in the field. Exposure to the people in an industry can be almost as valuable as industry experience itself. In addition to information and advice, it sometimes even produces job opportunities. **The value of networking cannot be overstated.**

CHAPTER 9
INVESTING, AND WHY IT MATTERS

Do you have the discipline to save
when it matters most?

If you've been using this book to help you fall asleep, please keep your eyes open during this chapter. Your long-term financial security might depend on it. For most recent graduates, investing isn't their first thought when waking up in the morning, nor should it be. But if you haven't thought about it by your second cup of coffee, you may want to revisit your routine. Just as you are never too old to stop learning, you are never too young to start investing.

Begin saving and investing now.

Now?! Yes, *now,* however modestly. There are two reasons for this. First, anyone under thirty, and maybe under forty, would be foolish to expect a "full" Social Security check once you reach the eligible age. Sure, you have been making contributions at (or since) your first job, but Social Security has one striking similarity to a Ponzi scheme (named after early twentieth-century con man Charles Ponzi). The funds paid out depend largely on new contributions (or 'investments' in Ponzi's scheme). **In the case of Social Security, the number of recipients is growing faster than the number of contributors, and Social Security payouts are unlikely to remain at current levels.**[19]

The second and more important reason for starting to invest early is **compound interest.** Compound interest is money earned on money earned. Sounds great, right? But what does it mean? Suppose that you were to save $1,000 every year until you retire at the age of 67. Let's also assume that you earn 5% in compound interest on those savings. Instead of earning $50 each year on each thousand dollars saved, you will actually earn more because of that "money earned on money earned." The money you save is constantly growing, constantly increasing your investment returns. But that's just a start. **Take a closer look at what can happen over the long-term.**

TOTAL SAVINGS AT AGE 67

(if you save $1,000 every year)

STARTING AT	"UNDER THE MATTRESS"	EARN 5% SIMPLE INTEREST	EARN 5% COMPOUND INTEREST
Age 20	$47,000	$103,400	$187,025
Age 30	$37,000	$72,150	$106,709
Age 40	$27,000	$45,900	$57,403
Age 50	$17,000	$24,650	$27,132

*5% may or may not be a realistic return assumption based on the current market conditions.
Calculations are based on a single annual contribution to your savings made on the first day of each year.
Simple interest payments are made on the first day of each year.*

If a picture is worth a thousand words, then the Total Savings table might be worth $106,709 to every thirty-year-old and substantially more if you are younger. That $106,709 represents the amount of money you will have 37 years from now by saving $1,000 a year and earning 5% compound interest.

But if you haven't already begun, what's the best way to start? **For many, the most straightforward approach to long-term savings is your employer's 401(k) plan.** Available to most working people, a 401(k) plan represents a great financial opportunity. One reason is that many employers match a percentage of the contributions you make to the plan. This employer match is additional "free" money—money that will earn money with compounding. Those matching contributions can result in dollar amounts considerably greater than those you see in the right column of the Total Savings table.

As surprising as it may sound, nearly 25% of adults have $0 in retirement savings, and each year workers across the country decline to participate in their employer-sponsored 401(k) plan.[20] **Not taking advantage of those matching-funds handouts from their employer is a mistake.** Just as nonsensical is never bothering to invest money contributed to a 401(k) plan. These are employees who join the plan and make contributions, but rather than invest the money, they leave those contributions in cash, earning little or no interest, dividends, or appreciation. Clearly, **not investing the money is also a mistake.** To understand why, revisit the **Total Savings** table on the previous page. In this example, the saver earned 5% interest on his or her savings. If you eliminate the earnings from interest (or stock dividends and appreciation), you might as well have kept the money under your mattress. **Remember the power of compounding, whatever the rate, and at the very least invest your 401(k) assets in an interest-bearing investment, or other investment with a potential for growth** (we're coming to that). There are plenty of options available; seek advice from an expert if you need assistance in selecting investments that are right for you. **More important, for those of you who have access to a 401(k) plan, we will only say this once. But please remember it forever.**

Contribute at least the minimum to gain the maximum matching funds from your employer.

While economists frequently reference the idea that there is "no such thing as a free lunch," the company match (if your company has one) is about as close as you will ever come to getting something for nothing. If your company matches some portion of your contributions (contributing, say, 50 cents for every dollar you contribute) up to 3% of your salary, contribute at least 3% of your salary. If your company matches a portion of your contributions up to 6% of your salary, contribute at least 6%.

Here's another important rule.

Never cash-out your retirement plans early.

There are substantial penalties and taxes associated with early withdrawals. They turn a winning investment into a loser. Except in the event of a true emergency, leave your retirement plan intact.

"I just bought a new car and paid cash for it. Since I only had $30,000 in my retirement plan, I cashed it out to buy the car. I figure I can get back to $30,000 in a few years."

— 31-YEAR-OLD WORKER

You're kidding?! Friends and family should not let friends and family make early withdrawals from their retirement plans to buy $30,000 cars. There are many things in life you can't control, so why mess up those you can control? **Saving and investing is a decision that you can control.**

CHAPTER 9 ½
INVESTING SUBSECTION— THE ROTH IRA

Do you have a Roth IRA? If not, why not?

The Roth IRA, established in 1997, is a relatively new (and exciting) way to save for retirement. Most high-school graduates have never been told that the next few years of their lives represent an opportunity to make hundreds of thousands of dollars. It's true!

Consider starting a Roth IRA today.

The Roth IRA offers tremendous benefits to young investors. The most important of these is a unique provision that allows you, after age 59½, to withdraw the funds 100% *tax-free*. Now, you might be thinking that 59½ is a long way off and that surely you can delay your retirement contributions for another year or so. Yes you can, but by choosing to delay you are missing a great opportunity. Thinking of waiting another year to start? Think again. Why?

"Because life passes in the blink of an eye."

— A COUPLE CELEBRATING THEIR 67TH ANNIVERSARY

Remember the hundreds of thousands of dollars you can make? Here's how:

INVESTMENT RETURNS
based on a long-term 4.9% annual return

STARTING AT	ANNUAL INVESTMENT	ANNUAL RETURN	TOTAL VALUE AT AGE 59½
Age 18	$3,000	4.9%	$405,019
Age 22	$3,000	4.9%	$323,559
Age 32	$3,000	4.9%	$176,690

ASSUMPTIONS
You invest $3,000 annually from age 18 until age 59½.
You don't withdraw a single penny until you are 59½.
Calculations are based on a single contribution made on the first day of each year.

As you can see in the preceding table, by starting to save at age 18 instead of age 32, you can earn an extra **$228,329** by age 59½ (assuming a 4.9% rate of return per year). More importantly, once you get to age 59½, this cash is 100% yours, tax-free. It's true; under current regulations, *you won't pay a penny in taxes on your Roth IRA gains when you withdraw from the account upon retirement.* Although some of the benefit is delayed, **the tax-free attributes are what make the Roth IRA such a valuable investment tool for young investors.** Other "qualified" retirement plans like the 401(k) do not offer this special provision. In the case of a traditional IRA, taxes could reduce your savings by tens of thousands of dollars when you're ready to use those savings. And by the way, the earnings from your Roth IRA savings won't be taxed each year along the way as they grow.

Now, let's assume that you choose to invest a portion of your portfolio in stocks (higher risk for a chance at higher returns), and instead of earning 4.9% annually, you now earn 6.5%.

INVESTMENT RETURNS
based on a long-term 6.5% annual return

STARTING AT	ANNUAL INVESTMENT	ANNUAL RETURN	TOTAL VALUE AT AGE 59½
Age 18	$3,000	6.5%	**$623,437**
Age 22	$3,000	6.5%	$474,001
Age 32	$3,000	6.5%	$230,245

ASSUMPTIONS
You invest $3,000 annually from age 18 until age 59½.
You don't withdraw a single penny until you are 59½.
Calculations are based on a single contribution made on the first day of each year.

By starting at age 18 versus age 32, and earning an average of 6.5% a year, you can earn an extra **$393,192** by the time you reach age 59½! If the calculations on investment returns catch your attention, by all means please take the time to learn more about the various investment options available. Chances are that someone in your circle of family and friends has investment experience. If not, there is a vast amount of information available on the Internet and at the library. (Yes, libraries still exist.) And check out *The Missing Second Semester,* devoted to investing.

For starters, **here are two simple rules to follow when it comes to investing.**

1. If you don't understand it, **don't do it.**

2. If the person explaining it doesn't understand it, **don't do it.**

Not understanding an investment does not mean you shouldn't take some time to learn about it. But do not invest until you do understand where your money will be and what it will be doing.

It's important to point out that there are ways to catch up if you don't start saving or investing at age 18, 22, or even 32. But the point remains the same: **the earlier you begin saving for retirement (or anything else, for that matter), the more you'll have and the sooner you'll have it.** With that in mind,

The best time to start saving is **now.**

If you haven't started yet, reconsider your inaction. Plan to fund your Roth IRA. At the very least, start saving today—maybe with what you might have spent on the latest must-have item *(Do I need this? Why?).* Make a plan—a simple plan—you can recite with ease (the next two short chapters may help) and start with small but real steps. **The sacrifices you find yourself making will prove minor, and they will pay off in a big way later.**

CHAPTER 10
A DEFINING MOMENT

Which path will you choose?

Here are possible timelines for good choices and poor ones. Although theoretical, they reflect various "real world" decisions that we might face. The intent is to paint a picture of good/bad decisions and remind us (again) that **present-day decisions carry future consequences.**

GOOD VS. POOR CHOICES

The decisions you make today will affect you for the rest of your life.

Purchases used car.

Accepts first full-time job. Starts 401(k) plan.

Saves on housing by renting with three friends. Opens Roth IRA with savings.

Regularly makes extra student loan payments.

Accepts part-time job and supplements income with weekend work.

GRADUATION	YEAR 1	YEAR 2	YEAR 3	YEAR 4

Declines full-time job (wasn't dream job). No employment prospects.

First full-time job. Ignores 401(k) plan recommendations.

Defers student loan payments and uses credit cards to maintain lifestyle.

Purchases new car.

Borrows another $100k for graduate school.

Has career flexibility as well as lifestyle flexibility because of smart choices made when younger.

Strong credit score and savings allow for great rate on first home purchase.

Student loans paid in full!

| YEAR 5 | YEAR 10 | YEAR 20 | YEAR 30 | RETIREMENT |

Excessive home purchase.

Living paycheck-to-paycheck. *Minimal savings, minimal security. Retirement unlikely.*

Still no savings.

CHAPTER 11
MORE WAYS TO SAVE

Do you want to build true financial security?

When it comes to saving more, there are three approaches: increase your income, reduce your spending, or do both. Most of us can't substantially increase our income in the short-term. Sure, you can supplement it by other means (multiple jobs), but for most of us, our current income is fixed. This leaves only one real option for getting serious about saving: eliminating unnecessary and wasteful spending. Regardless of your income level, remember a key point from Chapter 2:

Do not let your spending dictate your saving.

Saving is **not easy.** If it were, everybody would be doing it. In order to improve your chances of success, saving must be effortless and automatic. *Step 1* is to **create a budget.** We can hear the groans, but your budget can be simple; it doesn't have to be overly complex or involve lengthy research. Here's a sample you're welcome to use. Just fill in the numbers. Even if you use rough estimates, it is worth your time to complete a basic budget.

Completing this sample budget will give you a clear picture of your actual spending habits and will allow you to make an informed evaluation of your financial well-being and (often tough) decisions about expenditures. Make saving manageable and delineate between short-term goals (student loan repayment/car purchase) and long-term goals (investments/house/retirement). Furthermore, **keep your funds in an account that is not readily accessible.** This is the *"I just lost my job"* fund, not the *"I want to vacation in Mexico"* fund.

Expect **and prepare** for the unexpected.

MONTHLY INCOME

Salary

Additional Income

Total Income _____

MONTHLY EXPENSES

OBLIGATIONS

Student Loans

Credit Card Debt

Other Debt

Total Obligations _____

NEEDS

Food

Shelter

Utilities

Broken Car/Fridge/Ankle/Computer Fund

Clothing

Medical

Transportation

Retirement Savings

Other Savings

Total Needs _____

Total Obligations + Needs _____

WANTS

Smartphone

Excess Clothing and Shoes

Hobbies and Interests

Vacation Fund

Apps and Video Games

We talked about it in Chapter 2 and it's worth mentioning again: **Manage your expenses.**

Total Wants _____

Because life is full of the unexpected, caution and thoroughness in financial preparations is more than warranted. Because an event is unexpected doesn't mean it should also be unanticipated.

"There is no such thing as bad weather; [you] just need to have the right gear."

— AN AVID HIKER (AND CFO OF A LARGE INVESTMENT FIRM)

Have you ever tried to negotiate the price of an umbrella on the streets of New York City during a downpour? Suffice it to say, your odds of success in that negotiation are poor at best. The point is, **don't set yourself up for failure.** *You should build an emergency fund that includes three to six months of living expenses.* While that may seem excessive, you simply can't predict the future. Jobs come and go. Medical emergencies happen. As we'll observe in Chapter 12, you never know when the bottom is going to fall out of that old water heater. There are many aspects of life that are out of our control. If adversity does come your way—which it inevitably will—at least you will be prepared. The budget you just made is a key component of your planning and preparation.

Analyze your spending habits, and consider the small expenditures you make every day. A little here and there might not seem like much, but as they say, *a journey of a thousand miles begins with the first step.* These simple ideas can save you hundreds of dollars each year. Be creative.

"I've been looking for a job for nine months now with no luck. Some leads have developed, but nothing imminent. Don't tell my wife, but I still get my caramel brulée latte every morning. Sure, $3.40 is a lot to spend, but I can't imagine going without it."

— JOB HUNTER

Wow! In this case, a coffee a day keeps the savings away! Old habits really do die hard. This seemingly small expense amounts to over $1,000 a year. Does it really make sense to spend this kind of money when you don't have a source of income (namely, a job)? For that matter, does it really make sense to spend this much on your daily coffee even if you *do* have a job?

If you don't have it, don't spend it.

There are many ways to be sure you *do* have it; that is, there are many ways to save, some less painful than others. The following are just a few examples:

Instead of going out Friday & Saturday, pick one night.

Pack your lunch.

How about those subscriptions **you don't use?**

Quit smoking (you know it's time). The likelihood of better health and lower healthcare costs makes this a rare *win-win-win.*

A final word of caution. The ATM card or payment app we all carry is an incredible convenience; it has likely helped many of us in an emergency. But easy access to your cash can also be a temptation. Use these tools wisely, and in conjunction with the budget we talked about.

CHAPTER 12
PUTTING A ROOF OVER YOUR HEAD

Can you afford to purchase a house?
Does it make sense to do so?

Notwithstanding what you might have learned from your parents, grandparents, or college roommate about the virtues of homeownership, **the last decade has demonstrated that buying a house is not for everyone.** In many cases, it has proven quite the opposite. The dream of homeownership has become a financial nightmare for people across the country. You might have also (correctly) learned from your parents, grandparents, or peers, that *if something sounds too good to be true, it probably is.* During the 2008 financial crisis, adjustable-rate mortgages and zero-down payments proved to be just that for many Americans—too good to be true.

In a very practical sense, the roof on an apartment keeps you just as dry as the roof on a house. And those apartment walls will keep you just as warm as those of a new house. The advantages of renting are numerous, usually enabling you to save money. You don't have to come up with a down payment (20% of the purchase price), you aren't responsible for maintenance and upkeep, and rent is usually lower than a monthly mortgage payment on a comparable house.

Equally important to these cost savings, renting serves as a great learning experience for potential homeowners—one that will indirectly prepare you for the responsibilities of homeownership and its accompanying surprises. For instance, as a renter, you don't have to worry about how you're going to pay for a broken air conditioner on a hot summer evening (or if you live in Minnesota, that broken heater on a cold winter morning). A call to your landlord gets it fixed, often at no cost to you. This is certainly not the case if you own the home. When real money is involved, it is sometimes better to be involved indirectly (as you would be in the case of renting) versus being involved directly (as you would be if you owned the home).

Long term. Yes, renting is smart, now. But eventually you're going to want and even need your own house, aren't you? Not so fast. Maybe you will. Maybe you won't. It's unwise to jump to conclusions or make any major financial decisions without looking at the particulars and weighing the options.

If and when you start thinking about buying a house, begin with the knowledge that a house you buy as a home is *a place to live*—not an investment. Deciding to buy a house under the expectation that its value will only rise is a proven fallacy.[21] Be realistic.

Your home is a place to live, not an investment.

Homeownership is a very expensive proposition—one to be taken seriously. **If you can't afford a 20% down payment, you can't afford the house.** It's as simple as that. And you should stop right there.

For the sake of discussion let's say that Aunt Megan and Uncle Andy have generously decided to foot the down payment for you (although we'll leave undetermined whether it comes in the form of a gift or a loan—a big difference). Even then, it's essential to think through the realities of owning a house—specifically, the costs and responsibilities that first-time home buyers often don't anticipate. Homeownership is not for everyone. Rather, like most things in life, it is a decision that should be made only after carefully considering your unique circumstances. Owning, not just buying, requires a significant *time* commitment as well as money. The demands of your schedule, career, and lifestyle are critical factors in the decision. Homeownership is a tremendous responsibility, and if you are unprepared, it can be an unpleasant as well as expensive experience.

If you are thinking about buying a house, be sure that it's the right choice for your circumstances. Ask, does it make more sense than renting? Compare the pros and cons of owning and renting with respect to your actual life—not someone else's ideal lifestyle, or even your ideal lifestyle. Be honest. Be realistic. Carefully consider your future financial well-being before making any significant financial decisions. Sure, we all want what the next guy/gal has. What if, instead, we abide by the theory, again, that *less is more* when it comes to spending money that could be better used building financial security and freedom?

Before jumping into the homeownership pool, stick in a toe to test the water. If it's too cold, don't jump. Many homeowners never understand the true cost of owning a home until it is too late.

"My brother was considering buying a home. He qualified for a fixed-rate, 30-year, $150,000 home mortgage loan. With a 6% interest rate, he said it would cost around $900 per month or $10,800 per year. Having purchased a house three years earlier I explained that while yes, $900 might be manageable on his $50,000 salary, homeownership is much more than a monthly payment."

— BIG BROTHER

In this instance, was it a stretch to afford that $150,000 home? If so, how does this young man plan to pay for homeowners insurance, mortgage insurance, and property taxes? These three expenses can add hundreds of dollars per month to your mortgage payment.

What about:

Utilities

Homeowner's dues
(common in condominium developments)

The faucet that springs a leak

The air conditioner that just died
(always in the middle of summer)

Broken refrigerator

Washer & dryer

The crack in the driveway is getting bigger

Furniture

Lawn and garden care

This list goes on...

See? *It's easy to become "house poor."* Avoid this trap.

If you can't afford it, **you can't afford it.**

Rent a house or an apartment until you are certain that you can afford all of the obligations associated with homeownership. If you do own a home, the same rules apply. Understand your obligations, financial and otherwise.

Why you shouldn't take a home equity loan to go to the super bowl

Sounds pretty ridiculous, doesn't it? To think that someone would risk his/her home for an opportunity to attend the Super Bowl. Would you forgo long-term security and freedom for instant gratification? Some of you are probably nodding your head right now.

Let's face it, though; every now and then an opportunity comes along that is nearly impossible to resist. Your friends are going to Europe. Your team is going to the Super Bowl. That new car you've been eyeing just showed up at the dealership down the street. Even so, it's smart to know whether this so-called "experience of a lifetime" could become the mistake of a lifetime. Plug the numbers into your budget and your savings schedule. See the real cost. *Then decide.*

We've discussed preparing for possible emergencies. By the same token, if you also prepare for these once-in-a-lifetime opportunities, you will have the resources to afford the trip. (Remember our Physician's Assistant from Chapter 7?) Better yet, you won't be tempted to make a poor decision like borrowing against your home.

Done correctly, owning a home can be incredibly rewarding—something that most of us hope to achieve. Certain aspects of the federal tax code (for example, the mortgage interest deduction) make it even more appealing. But remember: a home is your home; it should not be viewed as an investment. In other words, don't expect to make money on your home. But, and it might seem like a contradiction, your home is likely your largest financial **ASSET**. And if you have a mortgage, it is likely your largest expense. With that thought in mind you can understand how easy it can be to become house poor. Tack on the unexpected expenses—they **WILL** occur—and all of a sudden you are forced to cut somewhere else or assume more debt to keep your head above water. Voila! You are officially house poor. If you are not certain about a possible expense, get someone to help you understand.

If you are contemplating buying a house that stretches your monthly budget, are you at the same time sacrificing your commitment to your monthly savings? Remember the power of compounded earnings on those same savings? Let your saving dictate your spending (in this case, the cost of your house), not the opposite. What about starting a college fund for the kids? Is buying a bigger home worth it if it means your children will graduate with six-figure debt? Talk about starting a step behind! At this point in the book it has become a cliché, but your choices *do* have consequences.

Afterthought

You might be asking yourself, "How do I know how much house is too much house?" Or, "How much house can I afford?" For a quick answer, revisit Chapter 2, and recall that the average American budgets 33% of his or her income for housing (house, condo, etc.). This is a good a starting point. Take into account your personal circumstances and adjust accordingly.

CHAPTER 13
THE LAST CLASS

Are you ready to start?

Imagine reaching retirement age with such high levels of debt that you simply cannot afford to retire. Believe it or not, more and more people across the country face this frightening scenario. There was a time when it was standard practice to eliminate debt before retirement. But for years our spending has increased faster than our salaries, and we have instead become a society dangerously dependent upon borrowing—borrowing that in many cases has been encouraged. Personal debt has steadily increased for many years. As a result, to make ends meet, *many Americans have been forced to postpone retirement* and/or accept a lower standard of living in retirement.[22] Overwhelming (but avoidable) financial obligations have left many Americans with no option other than to keep working.

Work because you want to when you are older—not because you have to.

Statistically speaking, most people earn their largest salaries in their 50s and 60s, which should, in theory, allow them to make their biggest retirement-savings contributions at those ages. Older Americans are carrying record level of debt into retirement, making it more difficult to take advantage of this "near retirement" savings boost.[23] As a result, they are missing out on the end-of-career savings which their peak salary years should make possible. Moreover, some who had retired are forced to go back to work because their financial numbers no longer add up. Debt levels of older Americans have been rising for two decades. This is not the path to follow. Tighten your shoelaces; the time has come to explore a different way. Would you rather spend your later years doing what you want (traveling, visiting children, grandchildren, friends, and maybe even working, on your own terms), or would you rather work *because you have no choice?* It's your future; take ownership and make the hard choices. If you *want* to retire at some point, you have to take action to make it happen.

Your financial future is your responsibility.

Rather than bemoan your situation, recognize that you have a lot more control than you might think. Put your nose to the grindstone, show up to work, and learn to live without relying on borrowed money. Make the right decisions today, so that forty years from now you won't be sitting on the porch swing lamenting to anyone who will listen: *"If I only knew then what I know now."*

The choices you make now have consequences.

It has been made clear throughout the pages of this book that the more financial planning you do and the more smart choices you make now, the fewer hard choices you will have to make (or be forced to make) when you are older. But how do you know if you are making the right choices? **How do you know if you are saving enough?**

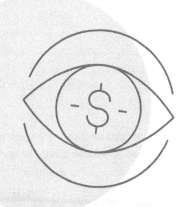

A first step is determining how much you need to save by the age of 65 so that you can meet your post-retirement income expectations. Here's a schedule that may help.

ESTIMATING HOW MUCH YOU NEED TO RETIRE

ANNUAL RETIREMENT INCOME	REQUIRED SAVINGS AT AGE 65
$20,000	$286,288
$25,000	$357,860
$30,000	*$429,432*
$35,000	$501,004
$40,000	$572,576
$50,000	**$715,720**
$75,000	$1,073,580
$100,000	$1,431,440

ASSUMPTIONS
Investment average rate of return = 5% (both before and after retirement).
Life expectancy: 90 years old. $0 balance on your 90th birthday (adjust accordingly if you plan to live longer).
During working years one contribution of $100 per month, made on the first of the month.
Once retired, one payout on the first of each month during the 25 years of retirement.
No further income or contributions after 65 (after all, you are busy enjoying retirement).

You can see from this table that if you want to have (or think you'll need) a post-retirement income of $50,000 a year, then you will need **$715,720** saved when you retire at age 65. Okay, but how do you know if you are on the right track?

The second and more important step is gauging how your savings stack up to where they should be at various points in your life. The table to the right uses the examples from the previous page to show the amount of needed savings at each age in order to reach the target annual income in retirement. The table shows that if, for example, you are 40 years old and expect to need $40,000 of annual income in retirement, you should have $147,295 in accumulated savings and investments.

CHECKING YOUR PROGRESS
Savings needed at various ages to reach annual retirement income targets

at age	Annual retirement income targets							
	$20,000	$25,000	$30,000	$35,000	**$40,000**	$50,000	$75,000	$100,000
	Savings needed to reach retirement target							
20	$8,768	$16,347	$23,926	$31,505	$39,084	$54,242	$92,137	$130,032
25	$18,081	$27,808	$37,534	$47,261	$56,988	$76,441	$125,073	$173,706
30	$30,03	$42,516	$54,999	$67,482	$79,964	$104,930	$167,343	$229,756
35	$45,373	$61,393	$77,413	$93,432	$109,452	$141,491	$221,590	$301,689
40	$65,059	$85,618	$106,177	$126,736	**$147,295**	$188,413	$291,208	$394,004
45	$90,323	$116,707	$143,092	$169,477	$195,861	$248,631	$380,554	$512,477
50	$122,746	$156,606	$190,467	$224,328	$258,189	$325,911	$495,216	$664,521
55	$164,355	$207,811	$251,267	$294,723	$338,178	$425,090	$642,369	$859,647
60	$217,756	$273,525	$329,295	$385,064	$440,833	$552,372	$831,218	$1,110,065
65	$286,288	$357,860	$429,432	$501,004	$572,576	$715,720	$1,073,580	$1,431,440

ASSUMPTIONS
Investment average rate of return = 5% (both before and after retirement).
Life expectancy: 90 years old. $0 balance on your 90th birthday (adjust accordingly if you plan to live longer).
During working years one contribution of $100 per month, made on the first of the month.
Once retired, one payout on the first of each month during the 25 years of retirement.
No further income or contributions after 65 (after all, you are busy enjoying retirement).

Based on your current age and total savings and investments, are you saving enough to provide the post-retirement income you need? This table can provide guidelines and a way to measure your savings. If you got a late start or are behind at any age, don't despair; it is possible to catch up. But a better approach, and the emphasis of this book, is to get ahead every step of the way.

There is a compelling reason why it's better to **arrive early** at each mile marker.

$1 of spending power today will not equal $1 of spending power tomorrow.

This is an important concept that **must be acknowledged and addressed in your plans.**

A formula known as *The Rule of 72* will help you prepare for the unfortunate reality that the dollar in your wallet will likely not be worth one dollar tomorrow. You can expect this trend to continue. Without going into too much detail, *The Rule of 72* is a very **simple formula that allows you to calculate how long it will take to double your money at various rates of return:** 72 divided by the rate = years to double. If you earn 5% annually on your investments or savings (assuming no additional contributions or withdrawals), you will double your money every 14.4 years (72 ÷ 5 = 14.4).

72 divided by the rate = years to double

The Rule of 72 can also be used to measure the effect of inflation: the rise in prices of everything that we buy (from cars to Q-tips) and the accompanying decline in the spending power of your savings. It will answer the question, "How much might $1 [or any amount] be worth in the future?" Between 1913-2020 inflation averaged close to 3.0% annually (more in some years, less in others).[24] *The Rule of 72* shows us that over this 107-year period, spending power has been roughly cut in half every 24 years. Remember the formula (72 divided by 3 = 24 years). In other words, one dollar of spending power today is likely to equal just fifty cents of spending power in 24 years.

So what does this mean if your present spending needs are $30,000 a year and you are 24 years away from retirement (or 41 years old)? If you expect to maintain the same "level" of spending in retirement, it means you should plan for $60,000 a year in savings thanks to the likelihood of inflation. This sounds scary, but let's quickly put it into context because it's highly likely your spending needs will be less in retirement. What do we mean? Remember from Chapter 12, *"if you have a mortgage it is likely your largest expense."* If managed correctly, paying off your home by the time you retire is a very achievable goal. Eliminating your *"largest expense"* is a sure-fire way to lower that post-retirement spending "level." You can do it. Adjust your savings accordingly, and put a little extra away whenever you can.

CONCLUSION
IT ISN'T LUCK

Do you have your seat belt on?
It's time to go to work.

If it's *"better to be lucky than good,"* isn't it funny how the more time we spend preparing, the *"luckier"* we generally are? A coincidence? Probably not! Financial reality can be a scary thing, but this book was not intended to frighten. Rather, it was designed to help you **prepare for the financial challenges that await.** What you get from this book should be just the first of many steps toward financial security.

Preparing to be "lucky"—making smart decisions and choices—means you can never stop learning about those choices and how to make them wisely. This concept goes far beyond formal schooling. Many successful people would suggest that your education is just beginning after you step into the working world. There is much to learn from reading, looking, asking, and listening. It's only smart to seek advice and guidance from knowledgeable people, people who have *"been there"* and *"done that,"* people with experience(s).

The late Norm Johnson, who graduated from Jamestown (NY) High School in 1939 and went on to an accomplished career in dentistry, had these words to share after celebrating his 91ˢᵗ birthday. Asked if after all his years, he had learned what there is to know about life, Norm smiled, folded his hands across his stomach, leaned back, and said, "The older I get, the more I become aware of just how little I truly know."

Wise words from a wise man, with the implication that *we never stop learning*. Norm Johnson represents a special generation, one that has a lot to share if we are willing to listen and learn.

At the same time, **don't expect help.**

Financial help is not on the way. Too often, too many of us expect something for nothing. Planning your financial future should *not* include an expectation that you will receive financial assistance from anyone. Expect only to be fairly compensated for the good work that you do. For a dollar's worth of work, expect a dollar of pay. Neither excuses nor entitlements will secure your future.

You are responsible for your action— and for your inaction.

As the gatekeeper for your financial security, there is only one person to blame for money problems, or to congratulate for financial success in the future. It's the person looking back in the mirror each morning. Make smart, disciplined choices, and that face will be a happier one.

Now, go do it. You're in charge.

ACKNOWLEDGEMENTS

We'd like to say a special thank you to all who made this book possible. To our panel of readers, friends and family who graciously offered their time, expertise and patience, thank you. To our editor, Stewart Smith, for challenging us and for helping us to greatly improve the quality of this book, thank you. To our cover designer, Brian Taylor, for the creativity and imagination that we lacked, thank you. To the team at Hunt Smith Design, for your hard work and commitment to this effort.

Lastly, and in this case, most importantly, to our wives: Whitney and Katie, for your patience, your love, and your support. **THANK YOU.**

With sincere appreciation and gratitude,

Gene & Matt

SOURCES

CHAPTER 1

1. 77% of Americans stressed
   https://www.capitalone.com/about/newsroom/mind-over-money-survey

2. 69% of Americans live paycheck-to-paycheck
   https://www.prnewswire.com/news-releases/number-of-americans-living-paycheck-to-paycheck-on-decline-despite-pandemic-301134207.html

3. 54% of American households spend more than they earn each year
   https://www.pewtrusts.org/en/research-and-analysis/issue-briefs/2017/03/how-income-volatility-interacts-with-american-families-financial-security

4. Student debt $1.5 trillion
   https://www.newyorkfed.org/medialibrary/interactives/householdcredit/data/pdf/hhdc_2019q2.pdf

5. 370% college increase
   https://nces.ed.gov/fastfacts/display.asp?id=76

6. Total credit card debt
   https://www.newyorkfed.org/microeconomics/hhdc.html

CHAPTER 2

7. 1.9 mm college students
    https://educationdata.org/number-of-college-graduates/

8. Average student loans
    *https://www.microcreditsummit.org/student-loan-debt-statistics/
    #:~:text=Student%20loan%20debt%20in%202020,consumer%20
    debt%2C%20behind%20mortgage%20debt*

9. Average unpaid credit card balance
    *https://wallethub.com/answers/cc/average-credit-card-debt-for-college-
    students-2140670817/#:~:text=The%20average%20credit%20card%20
    debt,2019%20Majoring%20in%20Money%20report*

10. Average salary
    *https://www.naceweb.org/uploadedfiles/files/2019/publication/executive-
    summary/2019-nace-salary-survey-summer-executive-summary.pdf*

11. Average American spending
    https://www.bls.gov/news.release/cesan.nr0.htm

12. After-tax salary
    https://smartasset.com/taxes/income-taxes#LH2DFAb8yc

13. Data suggest 20 years to pay off loans
    https://studentaid.gov/manage-loans/repayment/plans/standard

CHAPTER 5

14. 56-year calculation
    http://www.bankrate.com/calculators/managing-debt/minimum-payment-calculator.aspx

15. Average $6,200 credit card balance
    https://www.experian.com/blogs/ask-experian/state-of-credit-cards/#s4

CHAPTER 6

16. New car will lose 40% of its value
    https://www.carfax.com/blog/car-depreciation#:~:text=According%20to%20current%20depreciation%20rates,percent%20of%20its%20value%20annually

17. Benefits of a used car
    https://www.thebalance.com/buying-a-new-car-or-used-car-2385961

CHAPTER 8

18. Duration of first job
    https://www.expresspros.com/Newsroom/America-Employed/New-Survey-Results--Recent-Grads-Leave-First-Jobs-Quickly.aspx

CHAPTER 9

19. Social Security
    https://www.ssa.gov/policy/docs/ssb/v70n3/v70n3p111.html

20. 25% have $0 retirement
    https://www.federalreserve.gov/publications/files/2019-report-economic-well-being-us-households-202005.pdf

CHAPTER 12

21. Shiller, Robert J. *Irrational Exuberance, 2nd edition.* 2006.

CHAPTER 13

22. Retirement delay
    https://www.tiaainstitute.org/publication/understanding-debt-among-older-population

23. Debt in older Americans
    https://www.ncoa.org/economic-security/money-management/debt/senior-debt-facts/

24. Inflation data
    https://inflationdata.com/Inflation/Inflation/Cumulative_Inflation_by_Decade.asp

NOTES

Choices we make every day have financial consequences—in some cases, BIG financial consequences. Understanding these critical decisions requires understanding their long-term effects. *The Missing Semester* provides a short course on the essentials for making wise financial decisions and gaining financial freedom.

Although designed with the recent college graduate in mind, *The Missing Semester* is relevant to a much wider audience. Those who bypassed college, or who are already in the working world, may better relate to some of the topics discussed. For those still in college or high school, this is a chance to get a head-start on peers and an independent life.

The Missing Semester is based on **the principle of ownership**—ownership of your financial future. It begins with the premise that your financial future is your responsibility, and that you cannot plan for or expect help. The book shows how to build a strong financial foundation, prepare for the unexpected, and confront challenges.

The next step is *investing,* the focus of the next book in the series, *The Missing Second Semester.*

CPSIA information can be obtained
at www.ICGtesting.com
Printed in the USA
JSHW040911030322
23466JS00002B/2